P9-ECZ-889

The Bald Eagle

by Steve Potts

Content Consultant:
Sigrid Noll-Ueblacher
Birds of Prey Foundation

CAPSTONE PRESS
MANKATO, MINNESOTA

C A P S T O N E   P R E S S

818 North Willow Street • Mankato, Minnesota 56001
http://www.capstone-press.com

Printed in the United States of America.

Library of Congress Cataloging-in-Publication Data
Potts, Steve, 1956-
 The bald eagle/by Steve Potts.
 p. cm.--(Wildlife of North America)
 Includes bibliographical references (p.45) and index.
 Summary: Details the characteristics, habitat, and life cycle
of the bald eagle.
  ISBN 1-56065-546-1
 1. Bald eagle--Juvenile literature. [1. Bald eagle. 2. Eagles.]
I. Title. II. Series.
QL696.F32P69 1998
598.9'43--DC21

                                              97-5960
                                               CIP
                                               AC

Photo credits
Brian Beck, 21
Daybreak Imagery/Richard Day, cover, 41
William B. Folsom, 17, 32, 26
William Muñoz, 26
Root Resources/Stan Osolinski, 12
Lynn Stone, 6, 8, 10, 14, 18, 29, 30, 42
U.S. Fish and Wildlife/Sue Matthews, 22
Visuals Unlimited/Joe McDonald, 24, 39

Table of Contents

Fast Facts about Bald Eagles

Scientific Name: *Haliaeetus leucocephalus*

Height: The adult male bald eagle is about 30 inches (76 centimeters) tall. The female bald eagle is larger. Females grow to be about 40 inches (102 centimeters) tall.

Weight: Male bald eagles weigh eight to nine and one-half pounds (three and one-half to four kilograms). Female bald eagles are larger. They weigh up to 15 pounds (seven kilograms).

Physical Features: Bald eagles have a curved yellow beak and sharp claws called talons. Adult bald eagles have brown-feathered bodies. White feathers cover their heads and tails.

Range: Bald eagles live only in North America. Most bald eagles live in Alaska and Canada. Some eagles also live in Florida, Arizona, Colorado, Michigan, Minnesota, Oregon, Washington, and Wisconsin.

4

Habits: Some bald eagles migrate during winter. Migrate means to move from one place to another.

Food: Bald eagles eat fish. They also eat rabbits, turtles, ducks, geese, and other small animals. Sometimes they eat dead animals, too.

Reproduction: Female bald eagles lay one to three eggs in nests. Eggs hatch in 35 to 40 days.

Lifespan: Bald eagles live 20 to 30 years in the wild. They can live up to 50 years in parks and zoos.

Habitat: Bald eagles prefer living in areas without humans. They usually live near water. Many eagles make their homes near lakes and streams.

National Symbol: The bald eagle is the national symbol of the United States.

Chapter 1

The Bald Eagle

When people think of the United States, they think of the bald eagle. This is because the bald eagle is the national symbol of the United States. A symbol is something that stands for another thing. For many people, the bald eagle is a symbol of strength and freedom. The bald eagle's picture appears on currency, statues, and other things.

There are many different kinds of eagles. The bald eagle is found only in North America. Once there were many bald eagles in the United States. Today, scientists believe there are only about 5,000 bald eagles in the mainland United States. The mainland United States is every state except Hawaii and Alaska.

The bald eagle is found only in North America.

A bald eagle's wingspan helps it soar.

Kinds of Bald Eagles

There are two kinds of bald eagles. There are northern bald eagles and southern bald eagles.

Northern bald eagles live in the north. They migrate to warmer areas every winter. Migrate means to move from one place to another. Every summer they return to their nests. They use familiar landmarks to help them find their way. Bald eagles always return to the area where they were born. Scientists call this fidelity.

Southern bald eagles live in the warmer southern states. They do not migrate.

Appearance

The bald eagle is one of the largest North American birds. People can easily spot the bald eagle. Its pure white head and tail contrast with its dark brown body feathers.

A bald eagle's body is 30 to 40 inches (76 to 102 centimeters) tall. The bird's many layers of feathers make it appear larger. But it weighs only eight to 15 pounds (three to six and one-half kilograms). The bald eagle is so light because it has hollow bones. Most other birds also have thin, hollow bones. The bones are filled with air. This helps birds fly.

A bald eagle's wingspan is seven to eight feet (two to two and one-half meters). Wingspan is the distance between the outer tips of a bird's wings. The bald eagle's wingspan helps it soar. To soar means to fly very high in the air.

Flying

The bald eagle is a strong and powerful flyer. This is because of its large wings. The bald eagle uses thermals. Thermals are rising columns of hot

A bald eagle can glide for hours without flapping its wings.

air. The bald eagle rides thermals high into the sky. A bald eagle reaches speeds of 50 to 75 miles (80 to 120 kilometers) an hour when it soars.

Once the bald eagle is in the air, it uses its broad wings to glide. The bald eagle relies on air currents. An air current is a stream of moving air. A bald eagle flies into an air current. It stretches out its wings and floats on the moving air. It relaxes and floats along with the air current. This helps the bald eagle save energy. It can glide on the wind for hours without flapping its wings.

When flying, the bald eagle uses its tail to help it stay balanced. The tail also helps it change directions and stop.

Keen Eyesight

In the past, people who could see well were described as having an eagle eye. This is because all eagles have excellent eyesight. They can see three to five times better than humans. The bald eagle sees more colors than humans, too. This helps it hunt animals.

The bald eagle sees well because it has large eyes. Larger eyes give the bald eagle larger and clearer images. Each of the bald eagle's eyes moves separately. One eyeball can look to the right while the other looks to the left. This helps the bald eagle see many things at once.

The position of its eyes also gives the bald eagle better eyesight. Its eyes are in the front of its head. Its eyes face forward and slightly to the side. This helps the bald eagle see things in

front of it. Animals with eyes on the sides of their heads cannot easily see things in front.

Other Senses

The bald eagle does not hear as well as it sees. But it does rely on its hearing. The bald eagle hears the calls of other birds and animals.

Birds are different from most other animals. Their ears do not stick out from their bodies. This makes it easier for them to fly through the air. But it means that birds must turn their heads to locate sounds.

The bald eagle hears the calls of its young. It listens to the calls and warnings of other birds. Bald eagles also hear mating calls. Mating calls are high pitched and can be heard for miles.

Bald eagles do not have well-developed senses of taste or smell. They are not affected by taste or smell. This helps them eat many things.

Bald eagles hear the calls and warnings of other birds.

Chapter 2

Survival

The bald eagle is a bird of prey. This means it hunts and eats meat. Prey is an animal that is hunted by another animal for food.

The bald eagle eats from one-half to one and one-half pounds (220 to 675 grams) of food a day. It mainly eats fish. It will also eat rabbits, turtles, duck, geese, and other small animals. Sometimes a bald eagle will eat carrion. Carrion is the flesh of dead animals.

Hunting

The bald eagle hunts during the day. It usually hunts from a perch. A perch is a place where a

The bald eagle hunts and eats meat.

bird can rest. Bald eagle perches are usually high in the air and near water. A bald eagle can see a rabbit in a meadow almost two miles (three kilometers) from its perch.

Sometimes the bald eagle hunts from the air. It makes short flights from its perch. The bald eagle uses its keen eyes to spot prey. Then it flies low and snatches at prey with its feet.

Occasionally, the bald eagle will dive at its prey. The bald eagle travels at speeds of 125 to 200 miles (200 to 320 kilometers) per hour when it dives.

A bald eagle has claws called talons. Most talons are one and one-half inches (four centimeters) long. They help the bald eagle hunt. The bald eagle grips and snatches prey with its talons. Talons also help bald eagles defend themselves. It uses its talons as weapons against enemies.

The bald eagle's toes can stretch and bend. It uses its toes and talons to pick up and hold food. The bald eagle has small, rough bumps on its toes. These bumps help the bald eagle hold slippery fish.

Bald eagle perches are usually high in the air.

Fishing

The bald eagle has a special method of fishing. When it spots a fish, it dives down and brushes over the water's surface. It dips its talons into the water and spears the fish.

Sometimes the fish is too heavy for the bald eagle to fly with it to the perch. Then the bald eagle will swim the fish to shore. Its talons grip the fish to prevent the fish from escaping. The bald eagle is a good swimmer.

Usually, the bald eagle can catch fish without getting its feathers wet. The bald eagle also catches water animals such as ducks, geese, and turtles.

Sometimes the bald eagle steals food from animals and other birds. It often steals food from the osprey. The osprey is sometimes called the fish eagle.

The bald eagle swoops down on a flying osprey that is carrying a fish. The scared osprey drops the fish, and the bald eagle catches it. Sometimes the bald eagle uses its talons to snatch fish from the osprey.

Eating

The bald eagle carries prey to its perch. At the perch, the bald eagle eats its meal. Sometimes prey is very heavy. Then the bald eagle cannot carry it back to the perch. The bald eagle eats where it has killed its prey.

The bald eagle uses its beak to rip pieces of flesh from its prey. Since it has no teeth, the bald eagle swallows the pieces whole. It also swallows small objects such as rocks to help it digest food. These objects grind the food down in its stomach. They are called gastroliths.

Preening and Molting

The bald eagle cleans its feathers after it has finished hunting. It does this at other times during the day, too. The bald eagle uses its beak to arrange and clean its feathers. This process is called preening. An adult bald eagle has more than 6,000 feathers. Preening can take a lot of time.

Preening is important. Wind sometimes ruffles feathers. Feathers need to be smooth for the bald eagle to fly properly. The bald eagle uses its beak to smooth and clean each feather.

The bald eagle has a special organ near its tail. This organ produces oil. The bald eagle uses its beak to spread this oil on its feathers. The oil makes the bald eagle's feathers waterproof.

The bald eagle sheds and replaces all its feathers over two or three years. This is called molting. New feathers grow in to replace the lost ones. The molt takes place gradually, so the bald eagle can continue to fly and hunt.

Roosting

After feeding, bald eagles return to their roosts at night. A roost is a place where birds rest or build nests. Some bald eagles roost together. Bald eagles leave their roosts in the morning. They fly back to their feeding grounds.

A bald eagle uses its beak to preen its feathers.

Chapter 3

The Bald Eagle's Life

Some northern bald eagles migrate during the winter. Not all bald eagles migrate to the same place. They travel to places where there is a lot of food. They often hunt and eat in large groups.

In the spring, bald eagles return to their original homes. Then they are ready to begin courtship and mating.

Courtship

Male and female bald eagles do not mate until they are five years old. Once they do, they mate for life. They choose a second mate only if their first partner dies. Bald eagles have a time of

Some northern bald eagles migrate during the winter.

courtship before mating. Courtship is the attempts an animal makes to win the affection of another.

Male and female bald eagles do special flying displays during courtship. Whirling is one unusual courtship flying display. While in flight, a male and female lock talons. Then they tumble head-over-feet toward the ground. As they near the ground, they pull apart. Then they fly up higher and begin the process again.

Nesting

Bald eagles usually live near forests, lakes, and rivers. They choose places that are far from people. That way they will not be disturbed while they nest. Mating bald eagles build a nest called an aerie. They build their aeries in the tallest trees or on cliffs. The average height of the nest is 50 to 125 feet (15 to 37 and one-half meters) above ground. This helps bald eagles protect their nests. It also makes it easier for them to hunt.

Bald eagles spend many hours gathering sticks. For their first nest, the male and female build a small structure. It is usually three feet (one meter) wide and three feet (one meter) deep. They line the bottom of the nest with small branches or grass. They carry each branch to the nest and arrange it carefully. They often line the nest with small green branches and leaves, too.

Mating bald eagle pairs use the same aerie every year. Each year they make the aerie bigger by

World Record

According to the *Guinness Book of World Records*, a pair of bald eagles built the world's largest bird's nest. The pair lived in St. Petersburg, Florida. The nest was 20 feet (6 meters) deep. It weighed more than a ton (metric ton).

adding more sticks to it. Larger bald eagle aeries are about nine feet (270 centimeters) wide and 12 feet (360 centimeters) deep.

Each mating pair claims a territory around the aerie. They will attack other birds who enter it.

Eggs

A female bald eagle lays one to three eggs in early spring. These eggs are about three inches (seven and one-half centimeters) long. The female usually sits on the eggs to keep them warm. This is called incubation.

The parents take turns incubating the eggs. Sometimes the female flies off to eat. Then the male incubates and protects the eggs. The male and female incubate the eggs for 35 to 40 days. This is called the incubation period.

If an eagle's aerie is disturbed during the incubation period, the adults might fly away. The abandoned eggs become cold. If this happens, the young eagles may die inside the eggs. The eggs may never hatch.

The male and female guard their nest.

Eaglets

Young eagles are called eaglets. They hatch after 35 to 40 days. A thick layer of down covers newborn eaglets. This brown, fluffy coating keeps them dry and warm until they grow regular feathers. Regular dark brown feathers begin growing within three weeks after hatching.

The head and tail feathers stay brown until bald eagles are four or five years old. Then the head and tail feathers turn snowy white. Young eagles' eyes are brown and their beaks are black until the age of four or five. Then their eyes and beaks turn yellow.

Eaglets are helpless during the first few weeks of their lives. They cannot stand or walk in the nest. They cannot hunt for food. The adult eagles must feed the eaglets. The adults bring prey to the nest. They tear off tiny pieces for the eaglets. Feeding eaglets is a full-time job. Male and female eagles make many trips to the nest with food.

After several weeks, eaglets can move around the nest. Eaglets spend most of their time eating and resting. They also build up

After several weeks, eaglets can move around the nest.

their wing strength by flapping their wings and stretching them out. They play with sticks in the nest. They spend many hours each day preening their feathers, too.

Fledglings

A fledgling is a young bird that has just grown its flying feathers and is learning how to fly. Eaglets try to fly when they are about 10 to 12 weeks. Some bald eagles fly easily to a nearby tree or

rock. Then they return to the nest. A few eaglets may fly to the ground. Their parents will care for them until they become strong flyers.

Eaglets spend several weeks mastering their flying skills. They also learn how to hunt and feed. Sometimes eaglets return to the nest to roost or eat.

Some eaglets leave their home territory one or two months after they first begin to fly. They usually do not move too far. Then they begin a life on their own.

Migration

Eaglets are ready for their first migration in fall. Many eaglets die during this migration. Only strong eaglets are able to fly the long distance. Those that cannot have problems finding food in the cold weather. One out of eight bald eagles dies during its first year. The survivors usually live long lives.

Young bald eagles have feathers that are a mix of both brown and white. Bald eagles are not fully grown until they are four or five years old. Bald eagles in the wild usually live 20 to 30 years. Those that do not live in the wild may live to be 50 years old.

Young bald eagles' feathers are both brown and white.

Chapter 4

Past and Future

People have respected the bald eagle for many years. Native Americans felt the bald eagle was sacred. Because of this, many Native Americans believed that eagle feathers were special. Today, some Native Americans still believe this.

Some Native American groups still perform special eagle dances. This is how they honor the bird. Some people also tell stories about the bald eagle. The Lakota Sioux tell the following story about the eagle.

The Hunter Who Was Saved by Eagles
Once there was a very good hunter. He knew the ways of birds and other animals. One day he was

Eagle feathers are special to many Native Americans.

hunting far away from home. He looked up and saw two eagles flying. He stopped to watch them.

The hunter decided to climb a cliff to see the eagles better. At the top of the cliff, he saw two young eagles in a nest. The two parent eagles were circling above it.

The hunter made a rope and climbed toward the nest. But then his rope broke. He was stuck on the cliff. The hunter was afraid he would starve. He did not know what to do. Then he formed a plan.

He used the bit of rope he had left to tie a young eagle to each of his hands. He walked to the edge of the cliff and jumped. The eagles flew him to safety. The hunter thanked the eagles for their help.

United States Symbol

Native Americans were not the only people who valued bald eagles. Europeans who settled in North America also respected the bald eagle. When the settlers formed the United States, they wanted to choose a national symbol. No one could agree on what the symbol should be.

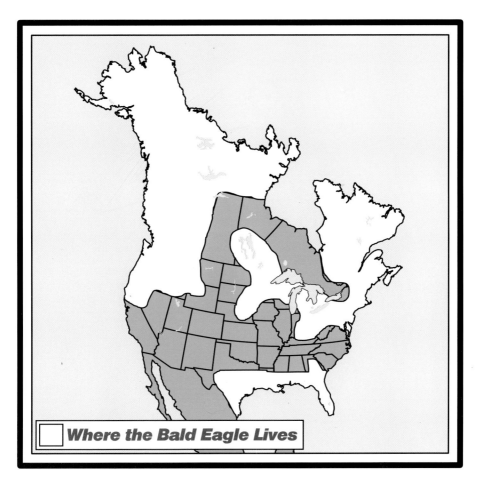

Where the Bald Eagle Lives

Benjamin Franklin was a famous inventor and leader. He wanted the wild turkey to be the national symbol. He wanted the turkey because it lives only in the United States. Bald eagles also live in Canada.

Other people wanted the bald eagle as the national symbol. These people felt the bald eagle was a powerful animal. Bald eagle supporters won the argument. The bird became the official symbol of the United States in 1782.

Past Dangers

Bald eagles were famous, but that did not protect them from dangers. The biggest danger to bald eagles was humans. Bald eagles have no known natural enemies.

Early settlers cut down forests that were home to bald eagles. They also hunted eagles for their feathers or for sport.

Modern science also proved dangerous to bald eagles. Scientists invented a powerful pesticide called DDT. A pesticide is a chemical poison used to kill insects that destroy crops. DDT damaged animal, bird, and fish life.

Birds and fish ate insects sprayed with DDT. Bald eagles ate the poisoned fish and birds. The poison hurt the bald eagles. It made female bald

The bald eagle is the national symbol of the United States.

eagles start laying eggs that had thin shells. The eggs cracked before eaglets were ready to hatch, and the eaglets died. By the late 1960s, only several thousand bald eagles lived in the wild.

The U.S. government banned DDT in 1972. Still, it continues to harm bald eagles. Scientists fear that it may take hundreds of years before DDT's harmful effects will completely disappear.

Today's Dangers

In 1940, the government passed the Bald Eagle Act. This law made it illegal to kill bald eagles. The United States placed the bald eagles on the endangered species list in 1973. An endangered species is an animal in danger of dying out. It is illegal to kill animals on the endangered species list. There are large fines and jail sentences for those who kill endangered species. Even so, many bald eagles are killed each year.

Some sheep ranchers shoot or poison bald eagles. They blame bald eagles for killing

Pesticides are in some of the fish that bald eagles eat.

lambs. Usually, bald eagles are not responsible for the lambs' deaths.

Other bald eagles die as a result of pesticides. The U.S. government banned many of the dangerous pesticides. Even so, the pesticides remain in the soil and water. Pesticides are even in some of the fish that bald eagles eat.

Electric power lines also kill many bald eagles. They often use power poles as perches. The high poles offer a nice lookout while hunting. But bald eagles die if they touch the wrong wires.

Bald eagles are also losing another battle. Many humans are building homes near lakes and rivers. This forces bald eagles to find other areas to live. Scientists worry that bald eagles will soon have nowhere to live.

Future

People are working hard to save bald eagles. It is now against the law to cut down trees that hold eagle nests. Only Native Americans can own or possess any part of a bald eagle. This is because bald eagles are important to many Native American religions.

Fines

People who kill or sell bald eagles illegally can be put in prison for one to two years. They may have to pay fines of up to $20,000.

Government protection helps the bald eagle. But concerned people can help the bald eagle, too. Every year the National Wildlife Federation sponsors a bald eagle count. Many volunteers help count

Scientists worry that bald eagles might soon have nowhere to live.

bald eagles. This helps scientists keep track of the bald eagle population. Then scientists can let the government know how well the bald eagles are doing. This work helps preserve the bald eagle's place in North America's wildlife heritage.

Large Wings

White Head

White Tail Feathers

Curved Beak

Brown Wing Feathers

Talons

Words to Know

aerie (AIR-ee)—an eagle's nest

carrion (KAIR-ee-uhn)—flesh of dead animals

fledgling (FLEJ-ling)—a young bird

incubate (ING-kyuh-bayt)—to sit on eggs to keep them warm

migrate (MYE-grate)—to move from one place to another

molting (MOHLT-ing)—a process in which birds lose their feathers and grow new ones

perch (PURCH)—a high place where a bird can rest and view its surroundings

pesticide (PESS-tuh-side)—a chemical poison used to kill insects

preening (PREEN-ing)—cleaning and arranging feathers

prey (PRAY)—an animal that is hunted by another animal for food

soar (SOR)—to fly high in the air

talon (TAL-uhn)—a long claw

thermal (THUR-muhl)—a rising column of hot air

To Learn More

Patent, Dorothy Hinshaw. *Eagles of America.* New York: Holiday House, 1995.

Patent, Dorothy Hinshaw. *Where Bald Eagles Gather*. New York: Clarion Books, 1994.

Ryden, Hope. *America's Bald Eagle*. New York: J.P. Putnam & Sons, 1985.

Sattler, Helen Roney. *The Book of Eagles.* New York: Lothrop, Lee & Shepard Books, 1989.

Van Wormer, Joe. *Eagles*. New York: E.P. Dutton, 1985.

Useful Addresses

Canadian Nature Federation
1 Nicholas Street
Suite 520
Ottawa, Ontario K1N 7B7
Canada

National Wildlife Federation
1400 16th Street NW
Washington, DC 20036-2217

Saving Bald Eagles Rescue Program
Earthwatch
680 Mount Auburn Street
P.O. Box 403
Watertown, MA 02272

U.S. Fish and Wildlife Service
Division of Endangered Species
Mail Stop 452 ARLSQ
1849 C Street, NW
Washington, DC 20240

Internet Sites

American Bald Eagle
http://www.cerf.net/mlc/Eagle.html

Bald Eagle—Facts
http://www.worldkids.net/eac/eagle.html

The Birds of Prey Foundation
http://www.birds-of-prey.org

Eagles.Org Home Page
http://www.eagles.org

Journey North
http://www.learner.org/content/k12/jnorth/1997
/critters/eagle

Index